Keeping The Peace:

A Church Member's Guide To CONFLICT Resolution

By
Pastor Michael S. Williams, D.Min.

Resource *Publications*
An imprint of *Wipf and Stock Publishers*
199 West 8th Avenue • Eugene OR 97401

©Pastor Michael S. Williams, D.Min. 1999
All Rights Reserved

This BOOK is intended for CHRISTIAN DISCIPLESHIP purposes *only*. It is an expression of the author's First Amendment rights, *should they actually exist*, under the United States Constitution. It is sold with the understanding that neither the publisher nor the author are engaged in the profession of providing advice in any manner, including, but not limited to: relationship counseling, therapy, psychological counseling, medicine, law, or any other manner of advice. **NOTHING** in this **BOOK** is intended to provide *any type of personal or professional advice*. If expert help is needed or desired, contact a competent professional. Any scenarios in this **BOOK**, *if* based upon actual occurrences, have been significantly altered. Any similarities between names, people, places, or situations posed within this book are merely coincidental.

Seventh Printing
The City Church Publication Society
San Francisco, CA

E-Mail Address: PMSW46@AOL.COM
Printed in the United States of America

WHAT OTHERS ARE SAYING ABOUT

Keeping The Peace: **A Church Member's Guide To CONFLICT Resolution**

Excellent! Excellent! Excellent!

Rev. Governor Johnson
San Francisco, CA

As a church officer, I find this book as a relief when it comes to orientating new members and resolving conflicts at the local church level!

Deacon Alfred Sellers
Chair, Board of Deacons
Saint James Missionary Baptist Church
San Francisco, CA

A rare masterpiece! I cannot see attempting conflict resolution in a church setting without this Biblically based guide at hand!

**Rev. Dorri Anderson
Pastor, Community Baptist Church
San Francisco, CA**

Again, my friend and colleague, Dr. Williams has written an easy-to-read guide for Christians everywhere!

**Mr. Lorenzo Lewis
Funeral Director
San Francisco, CA**

Dr. Williams is one of my favorite writers! This book is one of the many reasons why! I will never look at the causes and solutions to conflict in the same way ever again!

**Mr. Albert Valmore
Insurance Executive**

In my many years of pastoring, I have yet to run across a volume that deals with such a complicated subject in such an easy to read manner!

Rev. Joseph Harold, Jr.
Pastor, First Baptist Church of Parchester Village
Richmond, CA

Dr. Williams has provided an indispensable tool for all Christians, especially church officers! This book will fill a tremendous void! I recommend it to deacons everywhere!

Deacon Nathaniel Davis
Chair, Board of Deacons
Providence Baptist Church
San Francisco, CA

My friend, Pastor Michael S. Williams, has taken a complex and sometimes frightening subject, and put positive options into simple easy to read language!

Rev. John Brinson
Author of, *The Ministry of Deacons, Deaconesses and Mothers in Urban America*

As both a preacher and law enforcement official, I think Pastor Michael S. Williams' book is a rare find! I rely upon many of his insights in the course of my work!

Rev. Cordell Hawkins
Community Activist and Grief Counselor

My friend and colleague, Dr. Williams, has written an insightful and thought provoking book to and for Christians. This book urges Christians to put Christ first in their lives in order to resolve conflict!

Rev. Shad Riddick, DD
Pastor, Metropolitan Baptist Church
San Francisco, CA

TABLE OF CONTENTS

INTRODUCTION 12

TO HAVE A PROBLEM IS NOT THE PROBLEM! TO RECOGNIZE OR NOT RECOGNIZE THE SYMPTOMS OF THE PROBLEM –THAT IS THE PROBLEM! 27

THE USE OR THE BIBLE AS A PRIMARY SOURCE FOR CONFLICT RESOLUTION 46

VENGEANCE IS NOT MINE—IT'S HIS! 50

CONCLUSION 54

APPENDICES 59

JESUS AND JUDAS (APPENDIX A) 60

SIX STEPS TOWARD GETTING THE MOST OUT THE STUDY SECTION (APPENDIX B) 68

THE RESOLUTION DIAGRAM (APPENDIX C) 71

CONFLICTED CHARACTERS (APPENDIX D) 73

CONFLICT RESOLUTION MODES (APPENDIX E) 76

THE BUSINESS MEETING (APPENDIX F) 80

CONFLICT SCENARIOS (APPENDIX G) 82

BUSINESS MEETING ABUSE 83

LIVING PROOF THAT JUDAS IS ALIVE AND WELL 85

WHEN WISE GUYS COME TO WORSHIP	87
S/HE WON'T TAKE NO FOR AN ANSWER	89
MISCELLANEOUS SCRIPTURES	91
OTHER BOOKS BY DR. WILLIAMS	92
BIBLIOGRAPHY	93
ABOUT THE AUTHOR	96

An Early Conflict.....
and its
Resolution

A bram was very wealthy in livestock and in silver and gold. From southern Canaan he wandered until he came to Bethel, to the place between Bethel and Ai where he camped earlier and where he had first built an altar. Abram then called on the name of the LORD.

Now Lot, who was wandering with Abram, also had flocks, herds, and tents.

However, the land *could not* support them while they stayed together, for their possessions were so great that *they were not able* to stay together.

In addition, ARGUING arose between *Abram's* **herdsmen and the herdsmen of** *Lot…*

So *Abram* said to *Lot*, "Let there be no **FIGHTING** between you and me, or between your herdsmen and mine, for we are brothers.

Is not the whole land before you? *Let us GO OUR SEPARATE WAYS! If you go to the left, I'll go to the right; if you go to the right, I'll go to the left."*

Lot looked up and saw that the whole plain of the Jordan was lush and green, like the garden of the LORD, like the land of Egypt, toward Zoar. *This was before the LORD's destruction of Sodom and Gomorrah.*

So Lot chose for himself the entire Jordanian plain and set out toward the east. The two men parted company:

Abram lived in the land of Canaan, while Lot lived among the cities of the plain and camped near Sodom.

Now the *men of Sodom were wicked and were sinning against the LORD*. Genesis 13: 2-13 (MSW Paraphrase)

Introduction

This book is about a subject that can cause a great deal of embarrassment, it can also cause a tremendous amount of pride—*CHURCH* **CONFLICT**. It suggests some ways *CHURCH* **CONFLICT** can be *RESOLVED*. Since you are reading this book, there is a high probability that you have experienced one or more of the following:

- You have had "your" project or program rejected by your local church.

- A **MARRIED** church member cannot seem to keep **HIS** (or **a-hem** *HER*) hands or eyes off you.

- You have participated in, witnessed, or heard about *PUBLIC* **CONFLICT** in your local church. The results of the **CONFLICT**, depending upon the issue(s), egos, personalities, or stakes involved have sometimes resulted in friendships ending. Sometimes church **CONFLICT** can result in **PHYSICAL VIOLENCE** in the midst of a church business meeting, quarterly conference, the annual meeting of your district association or conference, state convention, annual conference, quadrennial meeting, national convention or convocation.

- You have participated in, or witnessed, *private* **CONFLICT** i.e., disagreement within the confines of the family. This type of **CONFLICT** can manifest itself in several destructive forms, regardless of the form's intensity. **CONFLICT** can manifest itself as **PHYSICAL, SEXUAL, EMOTIONAL,** or **FINANCIAL** abuse. *PRIVATE* **CONFLICT** can spill over into the *PUBLIC* **ARENA**. Do not fool yourself; one of the worst **PUBLIC ARENAS** can be the **CHURCH**!

The Christian's Role in CONFLICT Resolution

The Christian has only one of two options in the area of **CONFLICT**. The two options demand that s/he be either a source of the ***PROBLEM*** or that of the *SOLUTION*. There can be no:

- Middle Ground
- Straddling the Fence
- Hiding Heads in the Sand
- In-between

However, before we blindly rush in to "make peace,"

- Between the pastor and one of his associate preachers...
- Between another person and their "ex"....

- Between your niece and nephew....
- On your job....
- Between the ushers and the choir....
- Between the deacons and trustees....
- Between the "older" members of the church and the "new comers...."
- Between a husband and a wife....
- Between a man and a woman that were formerly "an item" and now have "broken up...."
- Between your child and his/her schoolteacher or work supervisor....
- Between your friend and his/her work supervisor....
- Between the pastor and a church officer....

You must have a clear idea as to what **CONFLICT** is.

What is CONFLICT?

For our purposes, **CONFLICT PRESUPPOSES A MINIMUM OF *TWO* OPPOSING IDEAS**.
- *I* say yes, *you say no....*
- *I* say only on 1st Sundays, *you* say only on 2nd Sundays....

- *I* say save, ***you say spend***....

- *I* say forget it, ***you*** say you cannot....

- *I* say *I* should be the district moderator, state or national president, pastor, deacon or trustee chairman, district superintendent, presiding elder, or bishop, and ***you*** say I'm not qualified....

NOW, LIST SOME OF YOUR OWN EXAMPLES

- _____
- _____
- _____
- _____

Why Appearances Are Not Always What They Seem

As we move to the next section, realize that the late Flip Wilson was only partially correct when he stated, **"WHAT YOU SEE IS WHAT YOU GET."** If you want to understand the nature of destructive **CONFLICT**, it must be understood that there is a difference between a **CONFLICT'S SYMPTOMS** and its **SUBSTANCE**.

CONFLICT: The Difference Between Symptom and SUBSTANCE

CONFLICT RESOLUTION or what *we think* is lava, and ashes—as terrible as it can be—is really

RESOLUTION, breaks down or fails because we confuse the **SYMPTOMS** of a particular **CONFLICT** with its **SUBSTANCE**! A **SYMPTOM** can be described as what we "see" on the **OUTSIDE**. The **SUBSTANCE** of **CONFLICT'S** is the **ORIGIN**. For instance:

- A volcanic eruption, with all of its poisonous gas, only the *SYMPTOM* of a disturbance **BENEATH** the earth's surface. The disturbance is the *SUBSTANCE* of the explosion.

- A spouse verbally or physically abusing the other is but a symptom of **SUBSTANTIVE *INTERNAL* CONFLICT**.

- An associate preacher or church officer that attempts to **PUBLICLY HUMILIATE** his pastor, by way of publicly pouting, scowling, or even denouncing the leader, has **SYMPTOMS** of **SUBSTANTIVE** problems relating to feelings of impatience and a lack of self-worth.

- Some *CONFLICTED TYPES*[1] wait until **SUNDAY** morning service to make **HIGHLY VISIBLE SYMBOLIC GESTURES, OR CONTROVERSIAL STATEMENTS**. They revel and thrive in making verbal, written, physical or otherwise, statements before the church family (*usually timed to make the greatest impact before the greatest number of people*). This type of person is showing symptoms of severe **INTERNAL** *SPIRITUAL* or even *PSYCHOLOGICAL* **PROBLEMS.** This person may have **UNRESOLVED INTERNAL CONFLICT**. A **BIBLICAL** example of **UNRESOLVED INTERNAL CONFLICT** was the strange set of parting instructions that David gave to Solomon while only a few hours away from death. David asked that Solomon exact bloody revenge upon people that had wronged him several years before. In one case, David had forgiven the person that

---

[1] A working definition of a *CONFLICTED TYPE* could go as follows: a *CONFLICTED TYPE* is a person that is a **SOURCE OF CONGREGATIONAL DISHARMONY**. That person has what are popularly known as "issues." These "issues" rage within them. These "issues" must be dealt with via **PRAYER, BIBLE STUDY, THERAPY, OR EVEN MEDICATION**—or a combination of all four, like the **VOLCANO**, they will erupt and **SPEW THEIR UNRESOLVED PAIN OVER ANY AND EVERYONE IN THEIR PATH!** The **BIBLE** is filled with examples of **CONFLICTED INDIVIDUALS**. God's people as shown in both **Old** and **New Testaments** are not immune from this problem. So as not to convey the impression that only *THEY* (*OTHERS*) can be sources of conflict within the church, realize that *ALL OF US* assume that role from time to time.

wronged him, but now that he was near death, he changed his mind (**1 Kings 2:1-9**)!

Examples of Conflicted Behavior in the Life of the Church

All too often we deal, or at least attempt to deal, with the **SYMPTOMS** of the problem, and not its **SUBSTANCE**.

We feel that if:

- If *I* were the pastor *instead* of Rev.___
- If *my spouse* would obligingly *die so I* could be "free"
- If *I* can gather enough support for *my* program
- If *I* can lobby the membership and have *them* "turn out" for the next meeting, and thereby have the vote "swing" in my direction
- If _____ would find *another* church to attend
- If the *pastor* would license or ordain *me*

- If *I* can "have my cake and eat it too"
- If *they* would re-elect me as _____
- If *my* spouse would not *provoke me* into "knocking him/her into next year"
- If *s/he* would just leave *his/her* spouse for *me*
- If an "a-hem," "unfortunate" accident were to occur, *I* could step into ____'s position. I could then be the_____
- If those low down dirty men/women would quit flirting with *my* _____

NOW, LIST SOME OF YOUR OWN EXAMPLES

- _____
- _____
- _____
- _____
-

THEN EVERYTHING would be as *IT,* (**In this case IT=THE WAY I THINK IT**), should be.

There are two things wrong with the above examples. First, they all focus in on the **SYMPTOMS** of **CONFLICT**; they ignore the **SUBSTANTIVE** reasons for **CONFLICT**. Second, notice—the person observing the discordant situation or person *NEVER* sees *HIMSELF* or *HERSELF* as part of the problem, it's always the *OTHER PERSON*.

When we concentrate on **SYMPTOMS**, we feel that by using **COERCIVE** measures, we can end the **CONFLICT** and everything will be "ok." In other words, if I:

- Bring a gun or a knife to business meeting

- Get so angry with Sister ____, that I could tear her to pieces after I beat the #*$%&^! @# Out of her!

- Come down the aisle for prayer or at the time of invitation, and slap, scream at, or expose the person I'm having a problem with

- Try to publicly humiliate the presiding officer of the meeting I'm attending by insinuating their lack of, sincerity, dedication or competence

- Make a deal to have enough support on hand to "declare the pulpit vacant."

- "Silence" my associate preacher

- "Sit the choir down"

- Get a restraining order

- Have legal papers served on the trustees **DURING WORSHIP**

- Get a court order to have the election of _____ voided

- Perform a "citizen's arrest" on Brother ____, especially during a business meeting or during a worship service

- Could get her to pay her child support

- Make him let me see my kids

- Get the police to get my neighbors to "pipe down"

…that all of **OUR** (translated **MY**) problems will literally disappear.

Make no mistake, sometimes measures such as the issuance of restraining orders or even institutionalization (i.e., incarceration), arrest, or physically distancing one's self from a destructive person or situation becomes necessary. However, we must realize that **EXTERNAL MEASURES** or that is to say trying to **COERCE** someone into behaving in a socially acceptable manner is at best a **SHORT-TERM** solution. **LONG-TERM** solutions involve being able to **RESOLVE CONFLICT**. This demands that we go beyond the **SYMPTOMS** of **CONFLICT**, and get to the **ROOT**, or **SUBSTANCE** of the problem.

GETTING TO THE ROOT OF THE PROBLEM MEANS GOING PAST:

- A person's *YELLING* and *SCREAMING*

- A spouse's *FLIRTATIOUS BEHAVIOR* with the wrong person

- An obstinate church member *PICKING AWAY* at every thing on the *BUSINESS MEETING AGENDA*

- Two stubborn board members literally at each other's throat complete with jugular veins sticking out while they vainly try to reach into their pockets to pull out their concealed weapons. They cannot get to them because other church members are holding them back. They are sweating and cursing each other and saying—**"LOOK YOU #@$%^,** you ought to be glad that we're in the church, **OTHERWISE I'D WHIP YOUR *&^%$#@!** [*Gluteus maxims*—or word's to that effect]. **NOTE**: During such instances, obscenities fly and rage. *The foul language usually refers to each other's thoughts concerning the allegations of promiscuous behavior on the part of the other person's mother as well as each other's beliefs concerning the other's sexual orientation.*

NOW LIST SOME OF YOUR OWN EXPERIENCES

- _____
- _____
- _____
- _____
- _____

Therefore, What is The "SUBSTANCE of CONFLICT?"

When we speak of the **SUBSTANCE OF CONFLICT**, we refer to the **ACTUAL CAUSE** of **CONFLICT**. I would suggest that the amount of destructive **CONFLICT** we experience in church is directly related to the quality of our relationship with the Lord (**1 John 2:9-11**). In other words, *MY RELATIONSHIP* with *you* will be no better than *my* relationship with *God.* Since we understand that our relationship with God must supercede all other relationships, then it stands to reason that if He commands our **DEEPEST** *SELF*, or *WILL*, we will be at peace with others.

The great Fourth Century African theologian, Saint Augustine, speaking of God, said in his *Confessions,*

> For You made us for Yourself, and our heart
> is restless, until it rests in You.

I would dare say that Augustine understood that there could be no peace with each other, until we are at peace with God!

The basic premise of this book is that **CONFLICT** even at its worse is **RESOLVABLE**. However, we must face it with an understanding that informs us—even demands of us—that we must go past **SYMPTOMS** and look at the **CONFLICT'S SUBSTANCE**.

The **BIBLE** is replete with examples of how different we are from God when it comes to understanding that **CONFLICT** doesn't start on the **OUTSIDE**, it begins on the **INSIDE**! This is why He is not impressed with what people think about us, because He realizes that humans always "judge a book by its cover!"

In fact, the **BIBLE** tells us that God's view of life itself is totally at odds with ours!

- *We* are impressed by what we see, *God* is not (**1 Samuel 10:20-23, 16: 6-7**)!
- *We* think that seniority should get priority; *God* does not (**Matthew 20:16**)!
- *We* are impressed by what people say, *God* is not (**Isaiah 29:13-16, Matthew 7:21-23**)!

- *You* and I think that persons *we* perceive to be acting in their own interests are our enemies. *God* does not (**Ephesians 6: 10-16**)!

- *We* think that our thoughts and plans are equal to *God's*; He says they are not (**Isaiah 55: 8-9**)!

- *We* think that we can bribe or manipulate Him into confirming our plans; *He* begs to differ (**Psalms 51:1-17**)!

Where does CONFLICT RESOLUTION start?

CONFLICT RESOLUTION begins with our personal relationship with God, not with the "problem" we perceive in the other person. The **RESOLUTION DIAGRAM (APPENDIX C** on **Pages 71-72)** gives a graphic example of how our **RELATIONSHIP WITH GOD** has a lot to do with our ability to resolve **CONFLICT.** To simplify matters, it shows us how our **RELATIONSHIP WITH OTHER PEOPLE**, Christian or not, is only as good as **RELATIONSHIP WITH GOD**.

In order to get the most out of this book, there are several basics you must "buy-into." They are as follows:

- All of us can from time to time find ourselves at *best* on **CONFLICT'S** "receiving end." At *worst, all of us* have been the vehicles of destructive **CONFLICT** at some point in our lives.

- God's people are not immune from internal **CONFLICT**, either personal or organizational
- God, through Jesus Christ is the ultimate peacemaker and keeper.

Keeping the Peace: A Church Member's Guide To Conflict Resolution presupposes four points. These points will unfold as chapters.

- To Have A Problem Is Not The Problem! To Recognize Or Not Recognize The Symptoms Of The Problem –That Is The Problem!
- The Use Of The **BIBLE** As A Primary Source For **CONFLICT** Resolution
- God as the Ultimate Resolver of **CONFLICT**.
- Conclusion

CHAPTER 1

To Have A Problem Is Not the Problem! To Recognize or Not Recognize The Symptoms Of The Problem –That Is The Problem!

During the Los Angeles riots, triggered by the vicious beating of Rodney King in the early 1990s, King asked a question that he hoped would stop the violence. He said—"can't, caaan't we all juuuust all git along??" His pleas were ignored and South Central Los Angeles burned for several more days.

At various times in the life of the church, we've all witnessed an old church mother, deacon, usher, preacher, moderator, bishop, state or national president beg warring factions within an assembly of Christians to:

- "Please stop the fist fighting!"
- "Why did you bring a gun to church?"
- "You two sisters should be ashamed of yourselves swearing at each other in business meeting!" To this the women may stop long enough to reply— **"SHUT-UP YOU OLD @#$%^&* before I COME UP THERE AND BEAT THE %$^&*$#$%!!! OUT OF YOU!" I'M FIXIN' TO TAKE CARE OF SOME *CHURCH* BUSINESS!**

- "Please refrain from fist fighting, that way the police won't have to be called and in turn arrest several of members!"

- "Who got the restraining order?"

- "Who told you to change the locks?"

Or sometimes an obstinate officer will say in a congregational meeting:

- "I'm not going to sign that *&%*^&$ check, I don't give a %*^&$#$#(% if the *church did vote* for that expenditure! I'm over the $! I have to save the church from itself! In addition, I will do it even if it means holding @#$%&*#$ Checkbook hostage!

- "What the %$%^^&*&*^% does the **BIBLE** have to do with this #$ %^**(^&*? We're gonna take care of some church business right now!

Church CONFLICT, CONFLICTED CHARACTERS and the Other Areas of Their Lives

It is impossible to be one person in one place and another elsewhere—unless you have a multiple personality disorder. It stands to reason that ***THE WAY A PERSON BEHAVES IN CHURCH IS HOW S/HE BEHAVES ELSEWHERE***! A person that has strained relationships with church members usually has strained relationships with co-workers, family members, and friends. **IF YOU**

ARE A MESSY CHURCH MEMBER, THEN YOU WILL BE A MESSY CO-WORKER, FAMILY MEMBER, STUDENT, ETC. Our behavior with our fellow believers will spill over into other areas of life. The only difference is that within the church context, you can't be:

- Written up...."
- Suspended....
- Have a reprimand placed in your **personnel file**....
- Be escorted out of the building *UNLESS THE POLICE ARE CALLED BECAUSE YOU ARE POSING A PHYSICAL THREAT TO YOURSELF AND OTHERS*...
- Have your security clearance "yanked...."
- Be expelled ....
- Or fired....

Within the **CHURCH CONTEXT**, you can:

- Pout if you don't get your way....
- Go on "strike" and refuse to participate in your auxiliary, sit in worship with an angry look on your face in order to get attention....

- Read a newspaper during worship, and when asked why, reply "if that @#$%&*@#$ preacher was sayin' somethin' worff hearin', I'd listen!"

Many of the worst church antagonists are intelligent enough to keep a lid on their disruptive behavior at home, work, and school. Why? Because they realize that foolish behavior can get them in trouble elsewhere! Nevertheless, on occasion, we do find exceptions. A colleague once told me of an incident that occurred in a church setting that he was familiar with.

> There was once a trustee that felt it was her mission in life to make the pastor's life a living hell. At every turn, she would take it as a God given responsibility to harass and humiliate the pastor. No setting was too sacred or inappropriate for her to be mean and spiteful towards the pastor. Well, the trustee finally ran into a problem. She had exhibited this type of behavior at work also. Her company was not bound by Christian principles and in due course fired her. She was in her mid-fifties and several years short of retirement. She had bills that had to be paid—but with no source of income, she was on her way to destitution. She found herself in the humiliating position of going to her pastor and begging for assistance in getting her job back. The pastor had mercy on her, referred her to a top-notch labor lawyer and got the trustee's job back.

CONFLICTED Church Personalities and Sexual Abuse

In their book, *Balm for Gilead, Pastoral Care for African American Families Experiencing Abuse*, Toinette Eugene and James Newton-Poling don't make a connection between home and church **CONFLICT**. However, they tell a heart-rending story of a young woman that was sexually abused by her uncle. The uncle, as well as his wife, was active members of their local church. The uncle was a member of the deacon board. The uncle and aunt also were members of the choir.[2] It is obvious that the uncle was a conflicted person at home. By extension, he may have been a conflicted church member.

CONFLICTED Church Personalities, Their Families and Congregational Politics

---

[2] Toinette M. Eugene and James Newton Poling, *Balm for Gilead, Pastoral Care for African American Families Experiencing Abuse* (Nashville: Abingdon Press, 1998), 76-78. Also see, Carrie Doehring, *Taking Care: Monitoring Power Dynamics and Relational Boundaries in Pastoral Care & Counseling* (Nashville: Abingdon Press, 1995); Marie M. Fortune, *Is Nothing Sacred? When Sex Invades the Pastoral Relationship* (San Francisco: HarperSanFrancisco, 1989); Stanley J. Grenz & Roy D. Bell, *Betrayal of Trust, Sexual Misconduct in the Pastorate* (Downers Grove, Ill: Inter Varsity Press, 1995); Carolyn Holderread Heggen, *Sexual Abuse in Christian Homes and Churches* (Scottsdale, PA: Herald Press, 1993); H. Newton Malony, *Clergy Malpractice* (Philadelphia: The Westminster Press, 1986).

Many of us have family members or friends that have lost respect for us and in turn walked away from the church, because they have seen us "in action," They have seen us,

- Gather enough votes in order to "kick the pastor out."

- Describe in vivid detail over the phone how we put those @#@#$%^& deacons, ushers, trustees, or preachers "in line."

- Drain the church's treasury due to legal fees because one group of members thinks that the vote at the last meeting was "rigged" therefore—'f-git the **BIBLE**, this is church business! I have the check book, let's go hire a lawyer."

List some examples of how **CONFLICT** in non-church arenas can spill over into the life of the church.

- _____
- _____
- _____
-

Many people leave an auxiliary, local church or denomination when they witness vicious **CONFLICT**. In some cases, they have been injured, physically, financially, emotionally, and sadly enough—spiritually!

It's sad but even the Christians that are fighting in the majority of cases, are not *evil* people. However, please realize that the ***absence*** of an ***evil intent*** doesn't prevent us from doing ***evil deeds*** and in turn reaping **harsh consequences**!

- Abram ***did not mean to*** cause Pharaoh trouble when he lied about Sarai being his sister, not his wife (**Genesis 12: 10-20**).

- Joseph ***didn't mean to*** anger his family by talking too much, but his intent didn't keep him from being sold into slavery by his brothers (**Genesis 37**).

- Moses ***didn't mean to*** become a fugitive from Egyptian justice after he committed murder; he obviously thought he was doing the right and just thing (**Exodus 2:11-15**).

- Saul disobeyed his pastor, Samuel, by not carrying out Samuel's command to its fullest. He even thought that he was doing Samuel a "favor" but the result was Saul's decline. Nevertheless, Saul didn't ***mean any harm*** (**1 Samuel 13: 8-14**).

What You See Is Not Always What You Get!

To many Christians, the absence of *o*-vert **CONFLICT** means that everything is going ok. Whenever a **CONFLICT** arises, they are the first ones to attempt to assume "mommy and daddy" role with the church. They will then attempt to "make peace" even to the point of getting between the warring factions and trying to get them to see that they should stop their fighting "for the good of the church." ***(They actually do this so that they can be seen as the saviors of the church—this is a very important role for them***).

However, what they don't know is that *co*-vert, or unseen **CONFLICT may be** brewing and just waiting for the right moment to explode. When the smoldering resentment/anger finally explodes, it comes as a great surprise and shock to those caught in the blast. Smoldering resentment can flare up even amongst those who voted "Yes" at "the meeting last night."

Smoldering Co-Vert Church Conflict, And Its Effects

Common church wisdom informs us that there are more meetings than the "formal" session. There can be meetings before and after. Dr. H. Beecher Hicks, Jr., pastor of Washington DC's famed Metropolitan Baptist Church, found this out the "hard way" when he attempted to lead his congregation in a massive renovation project in the late 1970s. In a book he wrote, aptly entitled, *Preaching Through a Storm*, Hicks relates:

> For the first four years of my pastorate, I found the board process to be as productive as it might be in any [church]. Then without warning, influential board members who had previously been models of responsible leadership suddenly and inexplicably turned hostile and uncooperative. It was the first sign of trouble to come.[3]

All too many times, we, like Hicks, are literally taken by surprise when **CONFLICT** arises. We do this because; we mistake a seemly **CALM EXTERIOR** with the *ABSENCE* **OF CONFLICT**. One of the greatest lessons I learned during my first pastorate was that for every single meeting I would chair, there were *several other meetings held prior to the official meeting*, as well as afterwards— *none of which I was aware of or invited to*. In addition, even if people voted in favor of a project, ***THAT DIDN'T MEAN THEY WERE FOR IT!*** So as a result, what I mistook for regular up front discussion and smooth parliamentary process really a deceptive calm in the midst

---

[3] Hicks goes on to describe three additional phases to the **CONFLICT.** They are as follows. Monies were embezzled. This served to undermine the confidence in the church's leadership. Second, a number of "concerned members" began to lobby for changes in the church's by-laws, i.e., creating various committees to "supervise" the pastor. Last, members of the surrounding community objected to any altering of the building, siting its "historic" character. They were able to have the local Committee on Historic Preservation and Landmarks to hold a hearing on whether the Metropolitan Church had the "right" to renovate their property. The Commission decided in favor of the Church. H. Beecher Hicks, Jr. *Preaching Through A Storm: Confirming the Power of Preaching in the Tempest of Church Conflict* (Grand Rapids, MI: Zondervan Publishing House, 1987), 36-38.

of a **CONFLICT** laden storm. Second, I found that even when people voted "Yes," that there would be an immediate meeting over the phone after the meeting or in the parking lot with people saying among themselves, "I don't know why we had to vote to _____. Things were fine the way they were!" Now, mind you—these same people voted "Yes" to the proposition! Why does this happen?

- Is it cowardice?
- Is it trickery?
- Is it because they didn't know what they were doing?
- Is it because their lives are so miserable that the very thought of positive change makes them nervous?

I really don't know. Maybe it was one of the reasons listed above, a combination of those reasons, or some I didn't list!

WHAT DO YOU THINK?

- _____
- _____
- _____
- _____

The Business Meeting as A Flash Point for CONFLICT

The "business meeting" has always served as a **FLASHPOINT** for people that want to "get things off their chests." This is especially true for African Americans. We have been disenfranchised by American society. We are constantly told in various ways that we "don't count." Even those whom we think have "made it" within the various professions may not be *as secure as we may think*. Many of our people feel that life has "passed them by." This makes them angry. Many of the worst church "hell raisers" I have known and experienced in a professional ministry that has spanned nearly thirty years feel powerless and disregarded by even those close to them. However, in church, they feel that they can be in "control of something." They may be **MENIAL LABORERS** at **WORK**, but at *CHURCH, THEY CAN BE SOMEBODY*. Where else can the a man or woman that has to mop floors at work, go home, shower and get dressed, and within two hours go to an institution (like the church) and refuse to cooperate? Even African Americans with "big time jobs" downtown, even with an impressive title, are sometimes the ones called to get *THE SANDWICHES, DONUTS AND COFFEE*, or to set the tone by singing *"ONE OF YOUR SONGS."* In other words, even if they do have an impressive title as well as a big office and all of the "perks" that go along with it, they could be, in actuality, the resident "darkie." *HOWEVER, AT CHURCH THEY CAN POUND THEIR FISTS ON TABLES AND DEMAND RESULTS*.

In the church, we can be what we never can be elsewhere! In addition, to be denied "power" or authority within the church can be seen as a direct challenge to that person's man/womanhood! As with any challenge, real or perceived, a reaction must come forth. The reaction is usually public in nature. In addition, as said earlier, it is usually designed to gain the maximum amount of exposure. In **APPENDIX F**, on **PAGES 80-81** you will find a **BUSINESS MEETING GRAPHIC** that describes the dynamics of destructive **CONFLICT** within the context of the church business meeting.

The **BIBLE** has several examples of votes going "one way" and then in due course, having the people act entirely different.

- The Israelites were glad that the Lord sent Moses to demand their release from Egyptian slavery, however when things didn't go their way, they complained (**See Exodus 4:27-31** *versus* **5:21, 5, Also, Exodus 14:10-14** *versus* **14:26-31-14, 26-31**).

- Joshua challenged the people of Israel to serve the Lord exclusively, and to stay away from other gods. The people enthusiastically voted to "serve the Lord." However, although Joshua warned them the Lord was not to be played with, they still voted to serve the Lord. Later their actions showed that they were not as serious as they thought they were, and consequently, the Lord had to chastise them (**Joshua 24:14-24 versus Judges 2:11-15**).

- Judas was one of the Master's closest disciples. He had charge of the $. His intimate fellowship with Jesus implied that he agreed with everything Jesus stood for. He even served as treasurer, however that position of trust did not keep him from becoming a **SNITCH** and **PAID INFORMANT**, as well as **STEALING** $ from the group (**Matthew 26: 14-16, Mark 14:12-16, Luke 22:7-13, John 12:1-6**)! He even summoned enough nerve to sit at table with Jesus the night of Jesus' arrest (**John 13:21-30**)!

Other Superficial Signs of Church CONFLICT

There are other "superficial," but no less important signs to be aware of. In his book, *Antagonists in the Church: How to Identify and Deal With Destructive Conflict,* Kenneth C. Haugk warns us to be on the "look out" for the following "red flags."

- If a person has been antagonistic in one congregation, look for them to behave in the same manner, or perhaps worse, when that person joins your congregation.

- If they are disruptive in other areas of their life, i.e., job, home, social clubs, etc., what makes you think that they won't behave in that manner when at church?

- They bring to you a list of grievances, because they "speak for some concerned" members." However, they refuse to divulge their identities.

- They constantly "down" your predecessor.

- They want to instantly become your "buddy," although they have just met you.
- They are gushing with praise for you, although they barely know you.
- They enjoy pointing out your "errors in judgement and weak administrative style" in public.
- They hop from church to church.
- They are consummate liars
- They employ underhanded ways to get what they want.
- They try to brow beat you with the fact that they are $ contributors to the church.
- They are constantly taking notes at inappropriate times
- They take the time to amass "evidence" against the object of their scorn. They collect anything attached to the life of the church, meeting minutes, old church bulletins, etc.
- They use sharp dagger like language in public and aim it at another person, all for the sake of humiliating that person.
- They do their "own thing," regardless as to what the church has decided.
- They are "pests."

- They believe that they are righteous in all of their actions.

- They are angry because things did not "go their way."

- They constantly "down" people that have not had the experiences that they have had. They constantly brag on how hard it has been for them, and how easy it is for the present group of "new-comers."[4]

CONFLICTED Biblical Characters[5]

One guaranteed way to "run people away" from a given church is for them to enter the fellowship of believers and then think that just because they are with Christians that there will/can not be destructive **CONFLICT**. Many long time Christians will witness destructive **CONFLICT** and fervently wish and pray that their church could be more like the First Century fellowship described by Luke in the **Book of Acts.** Luke records that on four occasions the body of believers was in harmony (**Acts 1:14, 2:1, 2:46, and 4:24**). However, this picture of loving unity has to be looked at over against the vicious infighting that has always plagued God's people. People that refuse to understand the grim fact that even God's people are subject to **CONFLICT** are

---

[4] Kenneth C. Haugk, *Antagonists in the Church: How to Identify and Deal With Destructive Conflict* (Minneapolis: Augsburg Publishing House, 1988), 69-79.

[5] See **APPENDIX D on Page 73.**

BIBLICALLY illiterate. A careful reading of the **BIBLE** will reveal that **CONFLICT** has and will break out, even among the people of God!

- The herdsmen of Abram and his nephew Lot **FOUGHT** over grazing land (**Genesis 13: 1-7**).

- Benjaminite tribesmen **RAPED** and **MURDERED** a Levitical priest's concubine after they could not engage in homosexual sex with him (**Judges 19-20**).

- King David, a "man after God's own heart," (**1 Samuel 13:14**) had a man **MURDERED IN COLD BLOOD** after having **SEX WITH and** getting the **MAN'S WIFE PREGNANT** (**2 Samuel 11-12**)

- The Disciples of Jesus were constantly **JOCKEYING FOR POWER AND AUTHORITY** over each other (**Matthew 20:20-28**). They even **BICKERED** among themselves the night of Jesus' arrest (**Luke 22:24-30**).

- The reason for the office of Deacon coming into existence was to quell **COMPLAINTS** between Greek speaking and Aramaic speaking Christians over allegations that the Greek speaking widows were bring left out when free food was being distributed (Acts 6).

- One of the reasons Paul was forced to write his first letter to the Corinthian Christians was due to divisions within the fellowship (**1 Corinthians 1:10-17**). At Corinth, it seems that Christians were not above **SUING** each other in civil court (**1 Corinthians 6: 1-8**)!

- Peter and Paul got into a heated **ARGUMENT** over a doctrinal issue (**Galatians 2:11-14**).

- There were some Christians that went out of their way to make Paul's life miserable (**2 Timothy 4:14**).

- A **SHOUTING MATCH** broke out among Jesus' Apostles over who was the greatest (**Luke 22:24**).

- False teaching caused a firestorm of **CONFLICT** over the issue of circumcision of non-Jewish male Christians (**Acts 15:1-11**, also see the entire book of **Galatians**).

- Paul and his close friend and traveling companion Barnabas parted ways after a **DISPUTE** over Paul's refusal to take John Mark along with them on a missionary journey (**Acts 15:36-40**).

- The Church at Corinth was torn by internal dissention due to **PERSONALITY CONFLICTS (1 Corinthians 1:10-16, 3)**, **INCEST (1 Corinthians 5:1-2)**, and **LAWSUITS** between believers **(1 Corinthians 6: 1-8)**.

Church Conflict, Preachers, $, And Leverage

Because their congregations pay the clergy, many insecure persons attempt to use this as leverage with their pastor. They forget, or neglect to think about the fact that their pastor may not be in the mood to be trifled with on a given day. In cases such as these, the pastor may lash out, maybe even violently (**2 Kings 2:23-25**). Some would be quick to say, "What a shame, he's acting like that! He's supposed to be our pastor!" However, persons that make such comments are usually the ones that provoked the controversy in the first place! A wise preacher will never lift himself above the rest of humanity by thinking that his call to ministry makes him immune to the hostility of the persons that he serves. That's why Paul's plead with the Lycaonians not to offer sacrifice to him and Barnabas, after they performed a miracle, is so relevant. Paul said, "… why are you doing this? We too are only men, *HUMAN BEINGS LIKE YOU*" (**Acts 14:14-15, NIV**). Later Paul's anger would boil to the point where he admitted to publicly rebuking Peter over a matter of doctrine (**Galatians 2:11-16**). Those that opposed his doctrine of salvation by Grace over against the Law **ANGERED HIM SO MUCH THAT HE WISHED THAT THEY WOULDN'T STOP**

AT CIRCUMCISION, BUT WOULD EVEN *CASTRATE* THEMSELVES (Galatians 5:12).

BIBLICAL Characters and CONFLICT

We can see then that even people that lived during **BIBLICAL** times were not immune from **CONFLICT** and controversy. If that's the case, what makes us think that we are immune? In addition, if we are just as prone to be embroiled in church **CONFLICT** and controversy, it behooves us to understand that the main problem with church **CONFLICT** is not that it is there! The main problem is that we are unwilling or unable to seek resolutions to our **CONFLICT**!

Now that we've seen that even the revered characters contained in the **BIBLE** were not immune from **CONFLICT and that** like the **BIBLICAL** characters we are prone to the same problems, let us now go to the **BIBLE** to seek solutions to **CONFLICT**.

Chapter 2

The Use or The BIBLE as A Primary Source for CONFLICT Resolution

I once taught a Christian Ethics class. I will never forget a comment made by one of my students. The student was engaged in a conversation with another student and me. The conversation centered itself around the topic of abortion. He was adamantly opposed to abortion. To buttress his opinion, he righteously exclaimed, "I have several scriptures to back me up!" To which I cautiously informed him that the **BIBLE** was not written to "back him up." Its main purpose was to witness to the sinfulness of the human race over against the Holy purposes of God! God's desire is for all to live in peace—under His Divine Rule. He has given all of us the opportunity to live in peace with each other after we have ceased our warfare with Him (**Ephesians 2:11-22**).

The **BIBLE** can be used abusively or in a liberating manner when it comes to **CONFLICT** resolution. An example of abuse could be the usage of the **BIBLE** to support injustice. A method of drawing upon the **BIBLE'S** liberating power can be found in paying careful attention to Jesus' words of warning to His Disciples. Before He sent them out on their "trial run," He shared with them the dangerous aspects of the journey. He said, "I send you out as sheep among wolves, therefore be *wise* as serpents, but *harmless* as doves" (**Matthew 10:16**). In the ancient world, the snake was looked upon as clever and cautious (**Genesis 3:1**). The dove was looked upon as a symbol of peace and the Holy Spirit (**Genesis 8: 8-12, Matthew 3:16**). In other words, the Christian is called to be *wise* and *Spirit* filled.

A good place to start looking for the wisdom aspect of the **BIBLE** is in the **Book of Proverbs**. Wisdom, according to the Scriptures, is to be sought after (**PROVERBS 1-9, James 3: 1-12**). In addition, according to **James**, God will give it to us if we ask for it (**James 1:5**). The Spirit's role in the matter is very comprehensive. Space will not allow us to be exhaustive. However, Paul's words are instructive relative to the role of the Holy Spirit in the life of the believer (See **Romans 8** and **Galatians 5: 13-24**).

Actual Conflicted Situations along with Various Methods of Resolution

Starting on **PAGES 76-79** (**APPENDIX E**), you will find five areas drawn from the **BIBLE** that can show us how to successfully navigate destructive **CONFLICT**. They are as follows:

- *Self Discipline* As A Way To Avoid Destructive **CONFLICT**
- *Avoidance Of Trouble* As A Method of Handling **CONFLICT**
- *Minding Ones Own Business* As A Way Of Avoiding Trouble
- *The Tongue* As A Blessing Or A Curse
- *Forgiveness*

A CAUTIONARY, AS WELL AS CONSTRUCTIVE WORD

As I grow in professional ministry, I find that the **BIBLE** is a multifaceted book. Not only is the **BIBLE** multifaceted, but we are multifaceted. In other words, we are all different. Since we are all different, the nature of the various conflicts that arise amongst believers will be different. Having said that, I would put forward the idea that **DIFFERENT *RESOLUTION*** processes must be used in **DIFFERENT SITUATIONS**. Most Christians are familiar with the process put forward by Jesus in **MATTHEW 18: 15-20**. That particular method was indorsed and encouraged by our Lord. However, since He is the **WORD,** and all **SCRIPTURE** is Divinely inspired for our benefit, then it would behoove us to take in the **WHOLE COUNSEL of GOD**, not just a section of it! Whatever method you use, it must be **BIBLICAL**! In addition, the Holy Spirit must lead you as you use any of the methods. Below, I have given you a sample list of scenarios and **BIBLICAL** responses. This list is by no means exhaustive; I encourage you to read the **BIBLE** yourself.

- Sometimes the best course could be to allow a **CONFLICTED PERSON** to have the first choice in the midst of a dispute. Usually they only end up hurting themselves (**GENESIS 13:8-13**).

- You may have to "call another person's bluff" (**1 KINGS 3:16-28**).

- Sometimes it's best to mind your own business and not get involved (**LUKE 12:13-16**).

- An excellent reason for not engaging an antagonist in either a **VERBAL**, to say nothing of **PHYSICAL,** contest is to not take what they say of do **PERSONALLY**! This is especially important for pastors to understand! If you have a truly God-given vision and your flock rejects it out of hand, don't take it personally, they are not rejecting you, they are rejecting God! In so doing, they are treading upon dangerous ground! (**1 SAMUEL 8:1-9**)! If they reject God, *THEY MUST PAY*! Nevertheless, the payment they must make cannot be of your doing! The *Lord will pay them back* (**2 TIMOTHY 4:14**).

An important lesson I've learned concerning dealing with conflicted characters is it is best to sometimes **LEAVE THEM ALONE** and let **GOD** handle them! We will explore that option in the next chapter!

Chapter 3

VENGEANCE IS NOT MINE—It's His!

During my developmental years, I received Godly, **BIBLICALLY** based instruction from my late grandmother. She would admonish me to allow God to "handle it." The "it" in question could have been anything from an unsuccessful scuffle on the school play yard to an act of injustice perpetrated against me within the context of ministry. I've been involved in ministry for nearly 35 years, and the wisdom my grandmother tried to impart to me is beginning to soak in. I would hope that it would not take you that long! The natural impulse is to "strike back" when attacked. However, through the power of the Holy Spirit and the prayerful reading of God's Word, we can successfully resolve at least our own internal **CONFLICTS** that want to link up with **CONFLICTS** contained within others. This section is for you, especially if you have been,

- Been victimized by **BACK ROOM** local church or denominational **POLITICS** that result in you not getting an assignment you hoped for.

- Deliberately **DOUBLE-CROSSED** by persons you thought to be "friends."

- Unjustly **FIRED**

- **OUSTED FROM YOUR PASTORATE**, in a very humiliating way, by a **PALACE COUP**. The conspirators are board members that were too cowardly to face you openly, or as individuals. No! **THEY MET IN SECRET** and came as a group to 'da meetin,' at which time you were voted out!

- A person with ***OBVIOUS PSYCHOLOGICAL*** disorders begins cultivating a "support group" to **AMBUSH** you in public.

Record Some Examples from Your Own Experience

- _____
- _____
- _____
- _____
- _____

I think that we get so caught up in "saving face" in the midst of what we perceive to be "defeat," especially after we feel that we've come out on the losing end after a humiliating "show-down," that we will become bitter and withdrawn. We will do this if we don't understand that the **BATTLE IS NOT OURS, IT'S THE LORD'S.**

Whenever we lose focus and forget this simple truth, we will become desperate and in turn act rashly. There is something about the American psyche that demands that we at least get the last "lick" in. After all, if we don't, we (think that) we will be perceived as weak or ineffective. However, in our own defense, who wants to be declared a "laughing stock?" Who wants to have to face the smirks of opponents that have seemingly "out maneuvered" you?

Sometimes you may even want to get "physical" with the person. Nevertheless, that could be unwise for several reasons.

- You could accidentally kill or seriously injure that person.

- You could be seriously injured or killed.

- You could act foolishly in front of a person that was going to "bless" you.

- You could be totally wrong.

- God may have had a worst punishment in store for the object of your anger, but you keep delaying your resolution or blessing because you just had to "save face."

The **BIBLE** is very clear on matters of vengeance. God warns us to not take matters into our own hands **(Deuteronomy 32:35, Psalms 4:4-5, Proverbs 24:17-18, 25:21-22, Nahum 1:2-7, Romans 12:20-21, Hebrews 10:30)**.

CONCLUSION

I took up a great deal of space writing of **CONFLICT** from its destructive aspect. However, was **BIBLE** believing Christians, we know that God can take the worst circumstances and make them redemptive.

- God called Abram to break his family ties and journey to a new land. By doing this, Abram would serve as the "Father of the Faithful," this would make it possible for God to redeem/save all that had/have faith in God (**Genesis 12:1-3, Romans 4, Galatians 3:1-14**).

- God allowed Joseph to be sold into Egyptian slavery in order to save his family from starvation (**Genesis 50:15-21**).

- Moses was a murderer as well as a fugitive from Egyptian justice. He also had a violent temper. However, the Lord chose him to lead the Israelites out of slavery. However, God had to prepare Moses for the task. God did this by making Moses serve as a shepherd, under his father-in-law Jethro's leadership for nearly forty years (**Exodus 2:11-17, 3:1-10**).

- God commanded one of his prophets to enter a humiliating marriage with a prostitute in order to show how Israel was unfaithful (See the **Book of Hosea**).

- Paul taught that the Lord could take our worst circumstances and bless through them (**Romans 8:32**).

The greatest miscarriage of justice ever perpetrated the crucifixion of our Lord, stands as the greatest example of God using negative circumstances to bless us! Without the **CRUCIFIXION**, there would have been no **RESURRECTION** from the dead on that first **EASTER** 2000 years ago. Without the **RESURRECTION,** we'd still be lost (**1 Corinthians 15:12-19**).

Finally, remember the next time **CONFLICT** breaks out in your local church that,

- As a Christian, you are either part of the solution or part of the problem.

- You need to be able to get past the symptom, and discover the **SUBSTANCE** of the **CONFLICT**

- Our relationship with each other will be no better than our relationship with the Lord.

- God has provided us His Word, written and in the Flesh, as well as the Holy Spirit in order that we can live the abundant life. Remember the words of our Master, "I came to give life in abundance (**John 10:10**).

Let us now get on with the mission of the church! That mission has nothing to do with,

- Summons being served on fellow Christians during worship

- Calling each other **$#%^&*#@#s** at business meeting

- Recounting the number of people that had to go to the ER after the last business meeting

- Vowing to "slap someone into next year" because they didn't vote to retain you as chair or president of your auxiliary

- Promising to "cut that **#$%%##$%^^'s** throat if s/he doesn't shut-the-**#$%^&*#** up and not sing that solo any more 'cause its mine!"

To the contrary, the main purpose of the church is to obey the Master's orders. Didn't He say,

"All authority in heaven and on earth has been given to me. Therefore go and make disciples of all nations, baptizing them in the name of the Father and of the Son and of the Holy Spirit, and teaching them to obey everything I have commanded you. And surely I am with you always, to the very end of the age." (**Matthew 28:18-20**).

Because of Calvary we can be reconciled

To God and each other!
(2 Corinthians 5:11-21 and Ephesians 2:11-22).

APPENDICES

JESUS and JUDAS (APPENDIX A)

Jesus and Judas, Handling Enemies: A Case Study

by
Pastor Michael S. Williams, D.Min.
PMSW46@AOL.COM

Section I

All of us, at one time or the other have found our selves facing down the "business end" of an enemy's mischief (**Acts 23: 12-21**) or we have *been* an enemy to an innocent person (**2 Samuel 11, Romans 3:23**).

Section I Notes

- _____
- _____
- _____

Section II

We can waste a tremendous amount of time trying to "change" an enemy, *on our own!*
- **Mark 5:1-6**
- **Ephesians 6:10-20**

Section II Notes

Section III

Judas' Relationship With Jesus

The relationship between Judas and Jesus furnishes us with an example/method of handling enemies.

- Judas was one of the "Twelve." He served as Jesus' treasurer (**John 13:29**).

- Judas was also a "White Collar" Criminal
  ✓ He was an embezzler (**John 12:1-6**).
  ✓ He was also a "paid informant." The "**AUTHORITIES**" *manipulated* his need for $, as well as his **fellowship with the DEVIL**, as a way to have Jesus arrested (**Matthew 26: 14-16, Mark 14:10-11, Luke 22:1-5**)!

Section III Notes

- _____
- _____
- _____

Section IV

Jesus' Relationship With Judas

Jesus, knowing all things, was well aware of Judas' treachery, but took no *apparent* action!

- Matthew 26:20-25
- Mark 14:17-21
- Luke 22:14, 21-23
- John 13: 21-30

Judas gains nothing but a motive to commit suicide! He **HANGS** himself (**Matthew 27:3-10**). *Jesus* **HANGS** from a cross, dies, is buried in a borrowed tomb, and rises on Easter Sunday morning!

Section IV Notes

- _____
- _____
- _____

Section V

What does this tell us? Several points, if we are willing to accept them!

- There is no need to seek revenge or to "pay some one back" for the trauma that person brought into your life! God is more than capable of handling it!
- The Father's children are expressly **FORBIDDEN** to seek justice on their own! Vengeance is God's!
    - ✓ **Proverbs 11:21, 20:22, 24: 14-18, 24:28-30**
    - ✓ **Romans 12:17-21**

- Evil has a tendency to destroy itself, it doesn't need our help (**Proverbs 10:21, 24, 11:21**)

- God can take the wrath of the wicked and allow them to "hang" themselves! (**2 Samuel 18:9-15, Esther 5:9-14, 7: 1-10**)
- It also helps to understand that "the battle is not yours, it's the Lord's" (**Exodus 14:13-14, Judges 7, Psalms 2**).

Section V Notes

- _____
- _____
- _____

Section VI

Finally, examine these two opposing views of dealing with enemies and ask yourself, how does my method compare with these views!

- There are some scores I *must* settle! I *NEED REVENGE*. I will not rest easy in my grave unless my bloody *REVENGE* is carried out (**1 Kings 2:1-9**)!

- I have people in my life that hurt me, but the Lord can/will handle them (2 **Timothy 4:6-14**).

Section VI Notes

- _____
- _____
- _____

ADDITIONAL SCRIPTURAL AIDS CONCERNING ENEMIES

✓ The **LORD** can cause your **ENEMIES** to be a **BLESSING** to **YOU** (**Genesis 37: 19-36, 50: 15-21**)!

✓ The **LORD** can take the **WORST CIRCUMSTANCES** and show you He is still in control (**Genesis 39: 2-6, 20-23, Romans 8:28**)!

✓ The **LORD** may arrange it to **REQUIRE** your enemies to **SEEK** *YOUR* intercessory help (**Numbers 12, 14: 1-20, Job 42:7-10**)!

NOTES

Six Steps Toward Getting the Most Out THE Study Section (APPENDIX B)

In order to get the most out of *Keeping The Peace: A Church Member's Guide To Conflict Resolution*, I recommend that you, or your group, follow six easy steps. *First*, read the **Pages 12-58**. As you read those pages, reflect upon the state of *your* fellowship with *God* and with *your* fellow believers. A possible option would be to appoint one of your group's members as a **STUDY LEADER** This person's duty would be to assign readings and role playing assignments to the group members from either the **Pages 12-58** or **APPENDICES B-F (Pages 68-80)**.

APPENDIX A, starting on **Page 60,** entitled *Jesus and Judas: Handling Enemies, A Case Study*, is a practical view of how *Jesus* handled His betrayer—*Judas Iscariot*. As Jesus handled Judas—so we can handle those that *deliberately* seek our harm!

Second, carefully study the **RESOLUTION ILLUSTRATION** contained in **APPENDIX C (Page 71)** before going on any further. The **RESOLUTION ILLUSTRATION** is designed to give you a view of **CONFLICT**, its **ORIGIN** and **RESOLUTION**, in an easy to read **BIBLICALLY** based manner. The diagram presupposes that our relationship with each other is no better than our relationship with God!

Third, carefully review **APPENDIX D (Page 73)**, entitled ***CONFLICTED BIBLICAL CHARACTERS***. Carefully read the Reference **SCRIPTURES** related to the **BIBLICAL** characters and the results of their **CONFLICTED BEHAVIOR**. Then think of modern day **CONFLICTED** characters and the **RESULTS OF THEIR BEHAVIOR**. List the results next the last column of the page.

Fourth, now it is time to explore various **METHODS** of **HANDLING CONFLICT in APPENDIX E** on **Page 76**. This section presents **FIVE METHODS** or **MODES** of handling conflict. They are as follows:

- Self Discipline
- Recognizing And Avoiding Trouble
- Minding Your Own Business
- Knowing How The Tongue Can Be Either A Blessing Or A Curse
- Forgiveness. This is related to *God's* forgiveness towards *us,* our forgiveness towards *each other*, and most importantly of our selves. This mode closes out with looking at the combination between our relationship with *God* and *each other*.

Fifth, Take a good look at **APPENDIX F,** the **Business Meeting Graphic**, on **Page 80**. That illustration will give you a basic idea of the level of political intrigue that goes on in the name of "the good (?) of the church."

Sixth, take advantage of the exercises in **APPENDIX G (Page 82)**. This will allow you to experience conflict in a "safe environment." This way, you may be able to recognize the "storm clouds" of destructive conflict prior to their arrival at your business meeting, charge or quarterly conference, district, state, or national meeting.

The exercises are as follows:

- **SCENARIO 1**. This situation is entitled, *When Giving In Is Not Surrender.*
- **SCENARIO 2**. This situation is entitled, *When It Is Best To Allow A Person To Hang Him/Herself*
- **SCENARIO 3** is entitled, *It's Not Good To Make The Battle With God A Personal Exchange Or Test Of Wills, He Will Always Get The Glory.*
- **SCENARIO 4** is entitled, *When S/He Won't Take No For An Answer.*

Last, but certainly not least, I have provided you with a **LIST OF SUGGESTED READINGS** of reading materials related to conflict resolution. Some are church related some are not.

THE RESOLUTION DIAGRAM (APPENDIX C)

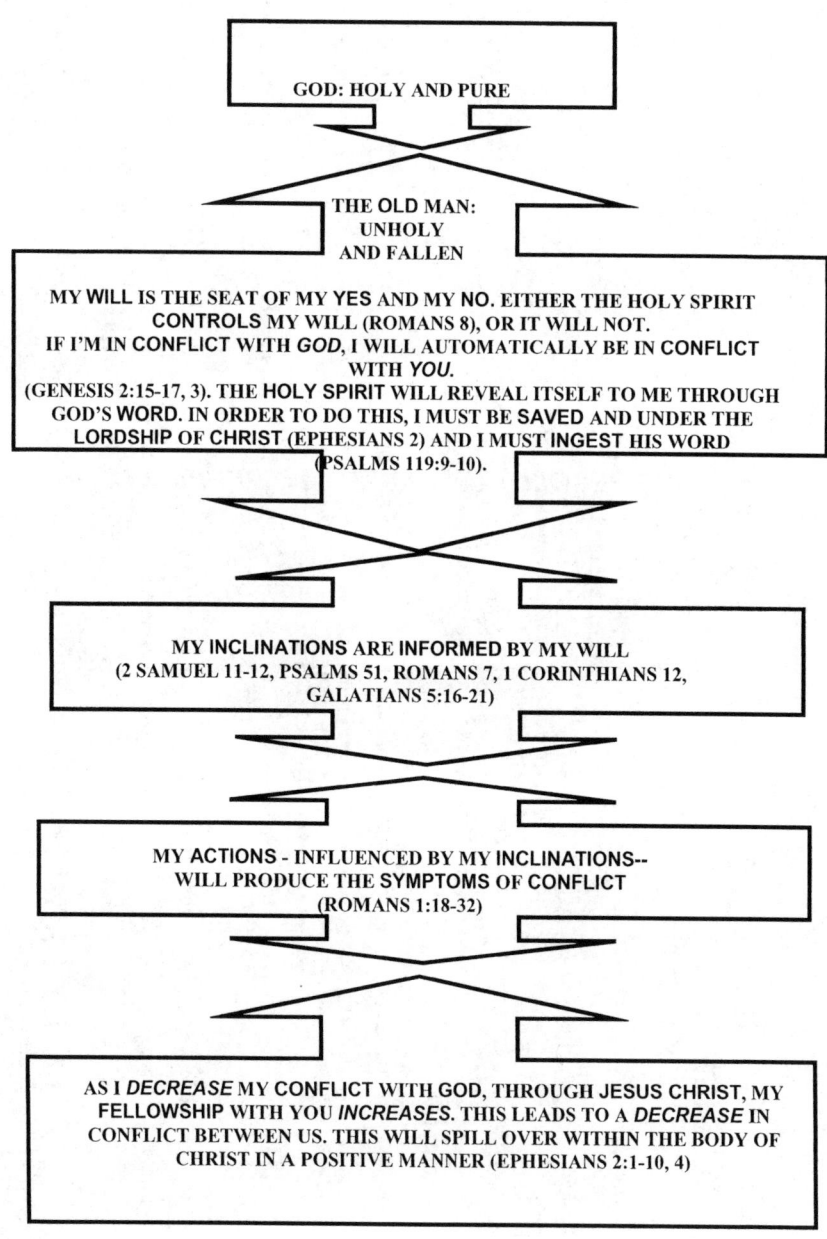

CONFLICTED CHARACTERS (APPENDIX D)

CONFLICTED BIBLICAL CHARACTER(S)	CONFLICT RESULT	CONFLICTED MODERN CHARACTER(S)	CONFLICT RESULT
Cain's Jealousy **Genesis 4:1-7**	*Murder* **Genesis 4:8**		
Jacob cheats his brother and tricks his father **Genesis 25:29-34, 27:1-40**	*Jacob flees for his life from his brother Esau* **Genesis 25:41-46**		
Moses murders an Egyptian **Exodus 2:11-14**	*Moses becomes a fugitive from Egyptian Justice* **Exodus 2:15**		
Jepthah is disowned by his brothers because his mother was a prostitute **Judges 11: 1-2**	*Jepthah becomes a bandit chief* **Judges 11:3**		
A rape/murder of a Levite's concubine by a group of Benjaminites **Judges 19**	*The entire nation of Israel is thrown into civil war because the Tribe of Benjamin refuses to extradite the rapists for trial* **Judges 20**		
David commits adultery with Bathsheba. **2 Samuel 11**	*David has the husband murdered. The Lord forgives David, but his family breaks down.* **2 Samuel 12-18**		

CONFLICTED BIBLICAL CHARACTER(S)	CONFLICT RESULT	CONFLICTED MODERN CHARACTER	CONFLICT RESULT
Judas spends the better part of his time with Jesus embezzling from the ministry. He even agrees to betray the Master for $ **Matthew 26: 14-16, Luke 22:5, John 12:1-8, 13:28-30.**	*Judas commits suicide.* **Matthew 27:3-10**		
King Herod Agrippa lusted after his niece. He wanted her so badly that he made a foolish public promise **Matthew 14:1-12**	*He has John the Baptist executed.* **Matthew 14:11**		
The Thessalonian Church has become certain lazy brethren's co-dependants **2 Thessalonians 3:6-13**	*Paul decrees that lazy persons are not to take advantage of the church* **2 Thessalonians 6:14**		

CONFLICT RESOLUTION MODES (APPENDIX E)

MODE #1	MODE #2	MODE #3	MODE #4
SELF DISCIPLINE	RECOGNIZING AND AVOIDING TROUBLE	MINDING YOUR OWN BUSINESS	HOW THE TONGUE CAN BLESS OR CURSE US
Proverbs 4:20-27 5, 10:17, 21 12:1, 13, 15 13:3, 10 14:3 15:18, 15:31-32 16:7, 16 16:32 17:10	Proverbs 16:6 18: 6-7 22:3, 24-25 29:9, 30:33 Titus 3:9-11 Matthew 4:5-7	Exodus 14:1-4 Proverbs 26:17 Luke 12:13-16	Proverbs 4:19 10:14, 19 11:12 14:29 15:1-2 16:28 18:6-7, 13 19:19 James 3:1-12

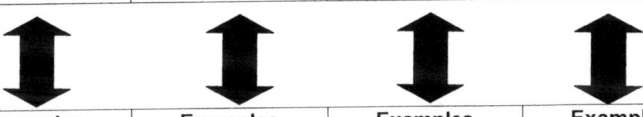

Examples	Examples	Examples	Examples

MODE #5	
FORGIVENESS & GOD	**FORGIVENESS & PEOPLE INCLUDING US!**
Psalms 25: 18, 78:17-55 2 Chronicles 6:22-31 Jeremiah 31:31-34, 36:1-3 Daniel 9:19 Amos 7:1-3	Matthew 18:15-20, 18:21, 18:23-34 Ephesians 4:25-32 Colossians 3:13

Examples	Examples

BOTH
Psalms 51 Matthew 6:21, 18: 35, 22: 22:34-40 Luke 15: 18 2 Corinthians 5:16:21 1 John 2: 7-11

GIVE EXAMPLES

THE BUSINESS MEETING (APPENDIX F)

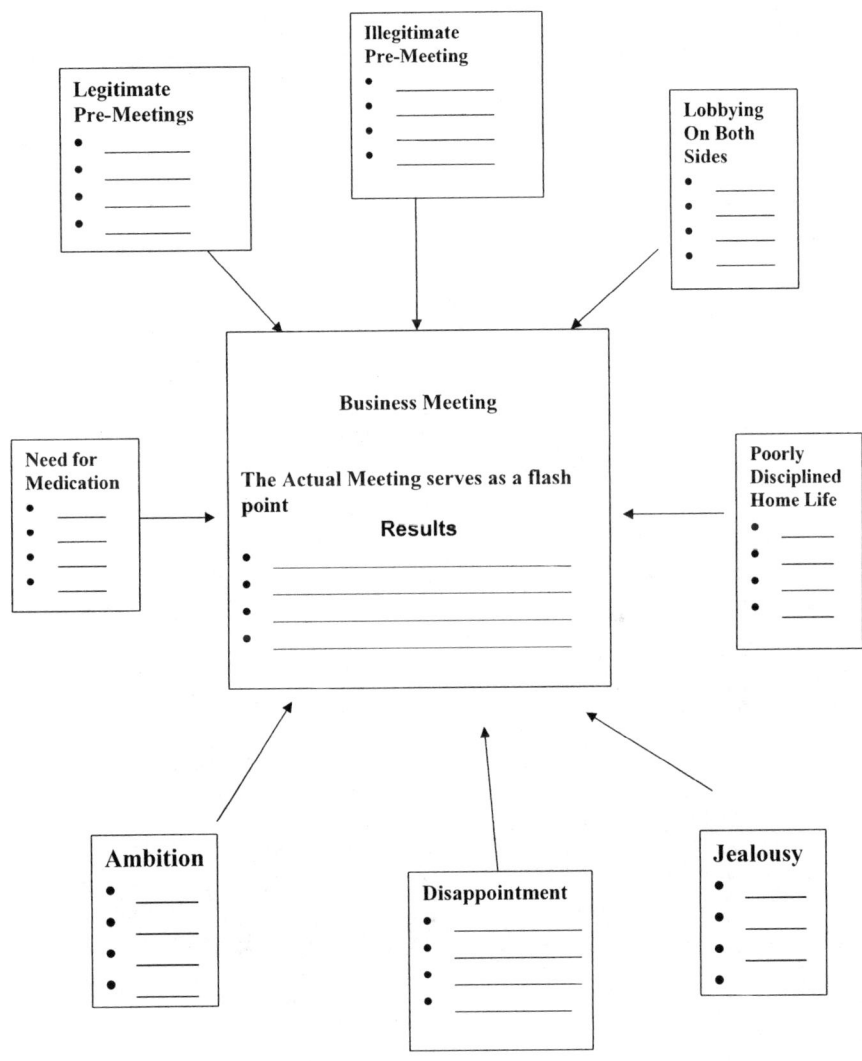

CONFLICT SCENARIOS (APPENDIX G)

Scenario #1

Business Meeting Abuse

Sister X has successfully lobbied the members of her "group" to effectively block the purchase of a piece of property directly across the street. The church is in desperate need of additional parking. She is a real estate agent (*with a suspended license*). She did not get to handle the sale, so she is angry. Through means most devious, she instigates a "call" meeting of the membership. With the people that came to the special "call" meeting, she succeeded in rescinding the previous congregational vote to acquire the property. She claims that what she did, she didn't do out of spite. To use her words, "I only did it for the 'good' of the church."

Which mode or combination of modes would you use?

MODE #1	MODE #2	MODE #3	MODE #4	MODE #5
WHY?	WHY?	WHY?	WHY?	WHY?
Desired Result	Desired Result	Desired Result	Desired Result	Desired Result

Scenario #2

Living Proof That Judas Is Alive And Well

Brother Y has successfully lobbied the membership, in the face of his pastor's opposition, to become a deacon. Brother Y is sneaky, underhanded, and a consummate liar. When he sits in front of the pastor during the sermon, he folds his hands and pretends to be sleep. He also purposely looks annoyed when the pastor makes his observations. When ever people join the church, he makes sure that they find out from him that the pastor is really "a low down and dirty @#$$%^&." There is an associate preacher at the church that Deacon Y has "buddied" up to. He and his "group" of "concerned" church members "wine and dine" the preacher. They flatter him and tell him that he would make a better pastor. In fact, they ask him, "Do you mind if we call you *pastor*? Since he is so eager to pastor a church, he readily agrees. The group plots and plans. They secure enough votes to oust the pastor at the next meeting. The vote is in dispute relative to the constitution; however, the pastor resigns in disgust.

Which mode or combination of modes would you use?

MODE #1	MODE #2	MODE #3	MODE # 4	MODE # 5
WHY?	WHY?	WHY?	WHY?	WHY?
Desired Result	Desired Result	Desired Result	Desired Result	Desired Result

Scenario #3

When Wise Guys Come To Worship

Brother G is the church's minister of music. He has deep family ties in the church. He can call out his support group at a minute's notice. The church's music department is his independent power base. He brags, "no one, and I mean no one can remove me, not even God!" In fact he has publicly stated in business meeting, choir rehearsal, private conversation that "I don't give *$%@#$%^&* what anyone says—even the Lord had better watch his step when it comes to the music department." He has some "shady" friends that are not above physically harming property or people if anyone crosses him! What can the church do?

Which mode or combination of modes would you use?

MODE #1	MODE #2	MODE #3	MODE# 4	MODE# 5
WHY?	WHY?	WHY?	WHY?	WHY?
Desired Result	Desired Result	Desired Result	Desired Result	Desired Result

Scenario #4

S/He Won't Take No For An Answer

Sister J feels that she is "in love" with Brother T. She feels that it is the "Lord's Will" that they get "together." After all, it has been *3 WHOLE MONTHS* since his wife passed. She feels that he is trying to thwart God's Will by not coming over to her house to eat dinner when invited. This is even after she tells him that she has purchased a "special outfit" for the "occasion." She even tells him "she always knew that one day they would get together." She is always in his face at church. She even stops by his job to give him a ride home, although he has a car. She even tells him, "I know that B (his late wife) would have us together! She came to me in a dream and told me so!" "Plus we were good friends while she was alive. When she was in the ICU at the hospital, even though she couldn't speak, I read in her eyes the following message; *I want you to marry my husband after I die*."

What should Brother T do?

Which mode or combination of modes would you use?

MODE#1	MODE #2	MODE #3	MODE# 4	MODE# 5
WHY?	WHY?	WHY?	WHY?	WHY?
Desired Result	Desired Result	Desired Result	Desired Result	Desired Result

Miscellaneous Scriptures For Conflict Resolvers

The following Bible verses will come in handy for various situations.

People That Talk Too Much: Proverbs 10:12, 18-20, 31; 11:9, 12-13; 12:19, 22-23; 13:3; 14:3, 16:28; 17:28; 18:6, 13, 21; 21:23, 28; 26:22
Messy People: Proverbs 10:23, 12:22; 14:7, 15:7; 17:4, 17:9, 14, 19-20; 22:8; 29:5, 22
Liars: Proverbs 12:19, 22
What Happens When You Don't Obey Godly Advice: Proverbs 13:13; 14:6
Why You Need To Listen To Your Pastor As He Leads You In The Way Of The Scriptures: Proverbs 13:16, 18; 15:5, 15:31, 16:21; 19:2, 20, 27-28; 23:12; Acts 5:1-11; 20:28; 1 Corinthians 11:1
Why It Is Dangerous To *DISOBEY*, Slander, Or Plot Against The Man Of God: 1 Samuel 12:6-15; 2 Kings 5:20-27; Jeremiah 3:15; Psalms 105:15; Hebrews 13:17
Staying Out Of Things That *Do Not* Concern You: Exodus 2:11-14 ; Proverbs 20:3; 22:10; 26:17

OTHER BOOKS BY DR. WILLIAMS

From Eden to Egypt: The Book of Genesis Revisited, 1999

No Rights and No Respect: A Documentary Commentary on African Life in America, 2000

Twisting in the Wind: The Anglo-American Legal Tradition and Africans In America, 2001

Bibliography

Baker, Benjamin S. *Shepherding the Sheep, Pastoral Care in the Black Tradition* Nashville: Broadman Press, 1983.

Bonhoeffer, Dietrich. *Life Together*. San Francisco: Harper & Row Publishers, 1954.

Brinson, John. *The Ministry of Deacons in Urban America, New Testament Church Origins of a Ministry of Compassion and Helpfulness.* Pinole, CA: Torchlight Publishers, 1994.

Cosgrove, Charles H. and Dennis D. Hatfield. *Church Conflict, the Systems Behind the Fights*. Nashville: Abingdon Press, 1994.

Ficken, Jock E. "Shielding Your Heart From Strife: Five Ways to Limit Conflict's Impact on You." *Leadership* 19:2 (Spring 1998): 27-30

Fields, Rev. Theodore P. *With Christ it Can be Done, A History of the First Twenty Years of New Hope Baptist Church of Union City, California.* El Cajon, CA: Christian Services Network, 1998.

Fisher, Roger and William Ury. *Getting to Yes, Negotiating Agreement Without Giving In.* New York: Penguin Books, 1982.

Haugk, Kenneth C. *Antagonists in the Church, How to Identify and Deal With Destructive Conflict.* Minneapolis: Augsburg Publishing House, 1988.

Henry, Jim. "Character Forged in Conflict." *Leadership* 19:2 (Spring 1998), 20-26.

Hicks, Jr. H. Beecher. *Preaching Through a Storm, Confirming the Power of Preaching in the Tempest of Church Conflict.* Grand Rapids, MI: Zondervan Publishing House 1987.

Lauterbach, Mark. "How I Realized That I Was Hurting People, and What I Did About It." *Leadership* 19:2 (Spring 1998): 31-33.

McCarty, C. Barry. *A Parliamentary Guide for Church Leaders*, Nashville: Broadman Press, 1987.

Massey, Floyd Jr. and Samuel Berry McKinney. *Church Administration in The Black Perspective.* Valley Forge: Judson Press, 1976.

McCarty, C. Barry. *A Parliamentary Guide for Church Leaders.* Nashville: Broadman Press, 1987.

McBurney, Louis. "North American Guide to Church Dragons, How to Identify and Approach Two Dangerous Species." *Leadership* 19:2 (Spring 1998): 34-38.

Payne, Leanne. Prayer When They Slander You, How to Call Heavenly Reinforcements for Earthly Battle." *Leadership* 19:2 (Winter 1998): 49-50.

Preston, Gary D. "Resisting the Urge to Hit Back: When Revenge Tempts You, Here's How to Forgive Completely." *Leadership* 19:2 (Spring 1998): 60-64.

Smith, T. Dewitt. *The Deacon in the Black Baptist Church.* Akron. OH: Church/Town Publications, 1983.

Smith, Wallace Charles. *The Church in the Life of the Black Family.* Valley Forge: Judson Press, 1985.

Walker, Clarence. *Biblical Counseling with African-Americans. Taking a Ride in the Ethiopian's Chariot.* Grand Rapids, MI.: Zondervan Publishing House, 1992.

White, Dr. R. L. *I Don't Need Counseling: I Ain't Crazy.* Lithonia, GA: Orman Press, 1998

Wise, III C. Dexter. *No Place for a Prophet, An Unconventional Preacher Trapped in a Traditional Church.* Westerville, OH: Wise Works, Inc., 1998.

About the Author

Pastor Michael S. Williams is a native of San Francisco, California. He is a product of San Francisco's public school system. He received his Bachelor of Arts degree *cum laude*, from Bishop College, formerly of Dallas, Texas, in 1976. He earned the Masters of Divinity and Doctor of Ministry degrees from the world-renown Pacific School of Religion, Berkeley, California in 1979 and 1996 respectively.

He served as the Assistant to the President of the Graduate Theological Union from 1996-1997 and holds dual membership with the American Academy of Religion and the Society of Biblical Literature. He also belongs to the Middle East Studies Association of North America. Pastor Williams holds the rank of Professor of Biblical Studies and Vice President for Development at the Southern Marin Bible Institute.

Pastor Williams has been in parish ministry for over a quarter century. He is a respected leader within his denomination, the National Baptist Convention, USA, Inc. and has served in a variety of pastoral and staff positions within the United Methodist Church, the African Methodist Episcopal Zion Church, the National Baptist Convention of America, and the National Baptist Convention, USA, Inc. He currently serves as Pastor of the Saint James Missionary Baptist Church of San Francisco, and Moderator of the Bay Area Baptist District Association.

Pastor Williams is married to the former Patricia A, Andrews. They are the parents of two children, Marthaa and Timothy.